Popular Classi

for Keyboard

Music arranged and processed by Barnes Music Engraving Ltd
East Sussex TN22 4HA, UK

Cover design by xheight design limited

Published 1996

Air (From Water Music)

By George Frederick Handel

Suggested Registration: Oboe
Rhythm: Soft Rock
Tempo: ♩ = 66

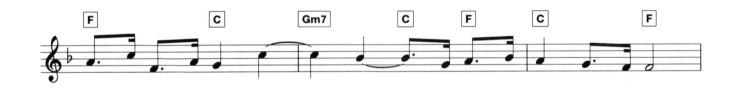

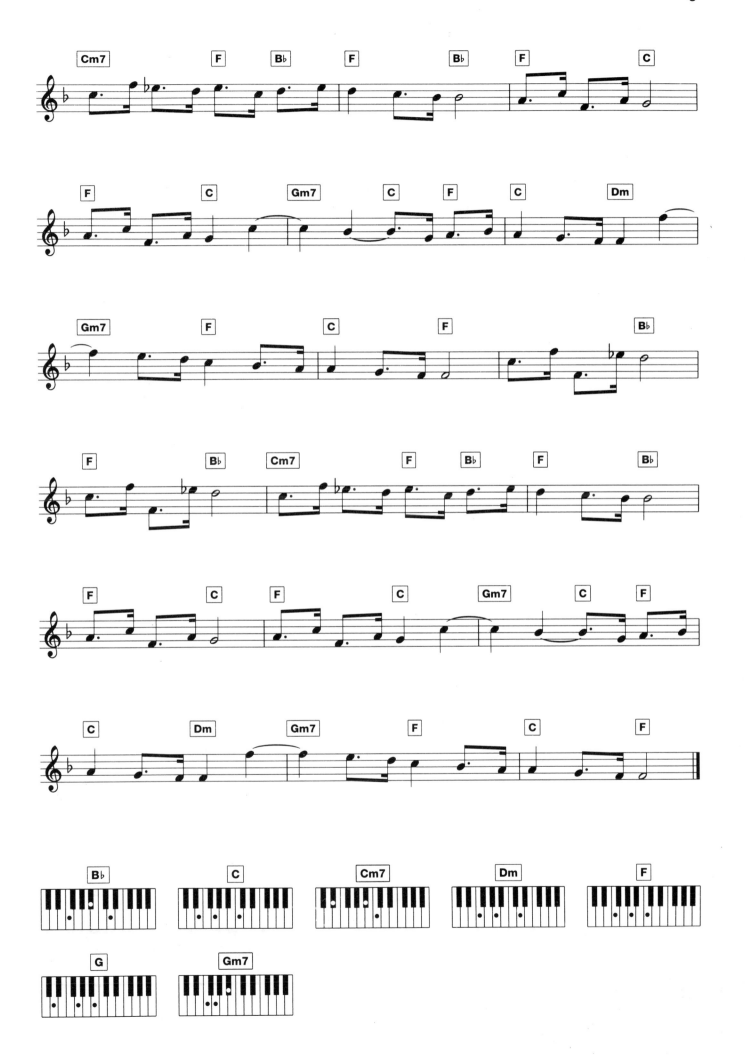

Air on the G String

By Johann Sebastian Bach

Suggested Registration: Strings
Rhythm: Soft Rock
Tempo: ♩ = 72

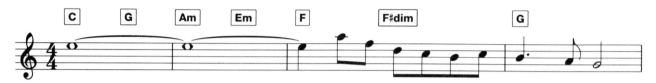

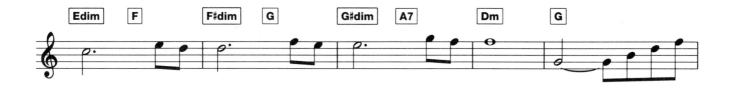

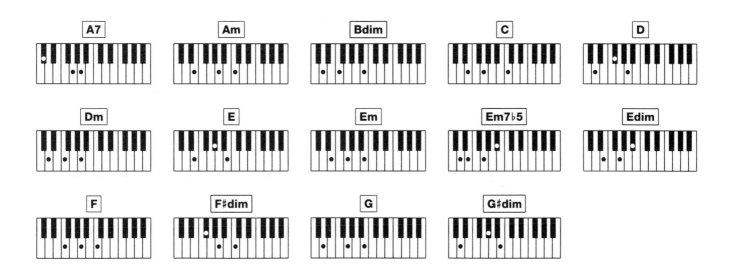

Can-Can
(From La Vie Parisienne)

By Jacques Offenbach

Suggested Registration: Accordian
Rhythm: March
Tempo: ♩ = 138

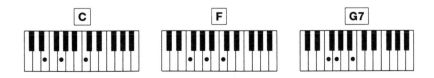

Concerto No 1 (Main Theme)

By Peter Ilyitch Tchaikovsky

Suggested Registration: Piano
Rhythm: Waltz
Tempo: ♩ = 84

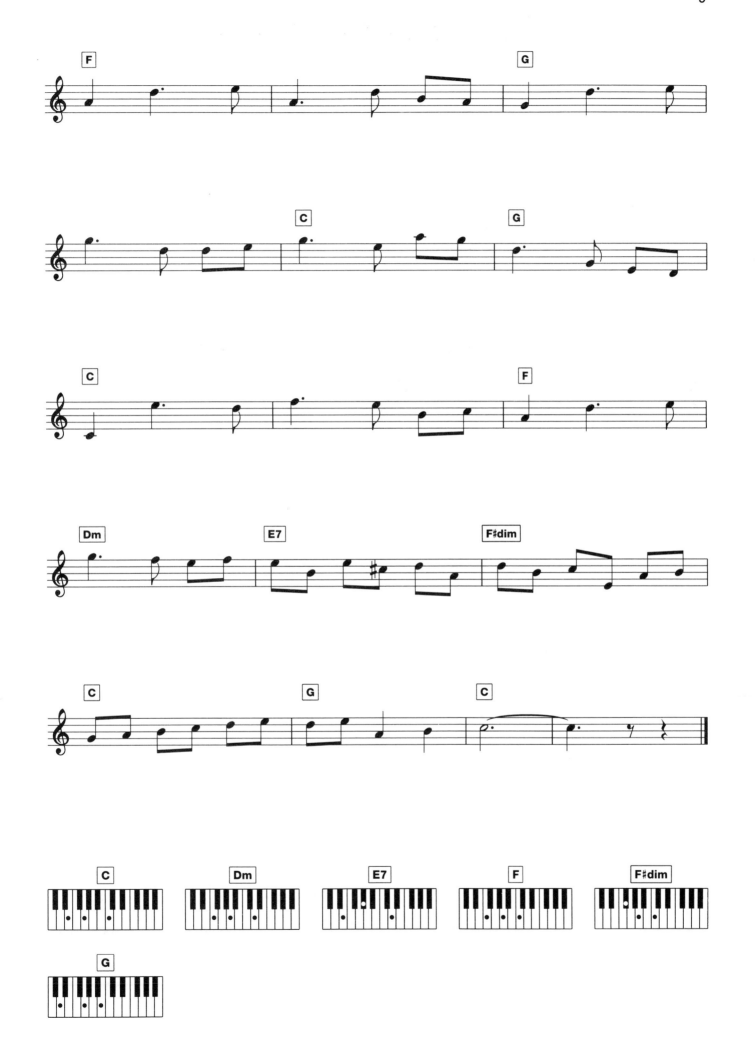

FANTASIE-IMPROMPTU

By Frederic François Chopin

Suggested Registration: Piano
Rhythm: Soft Rock
Tempo: ♩ = 96

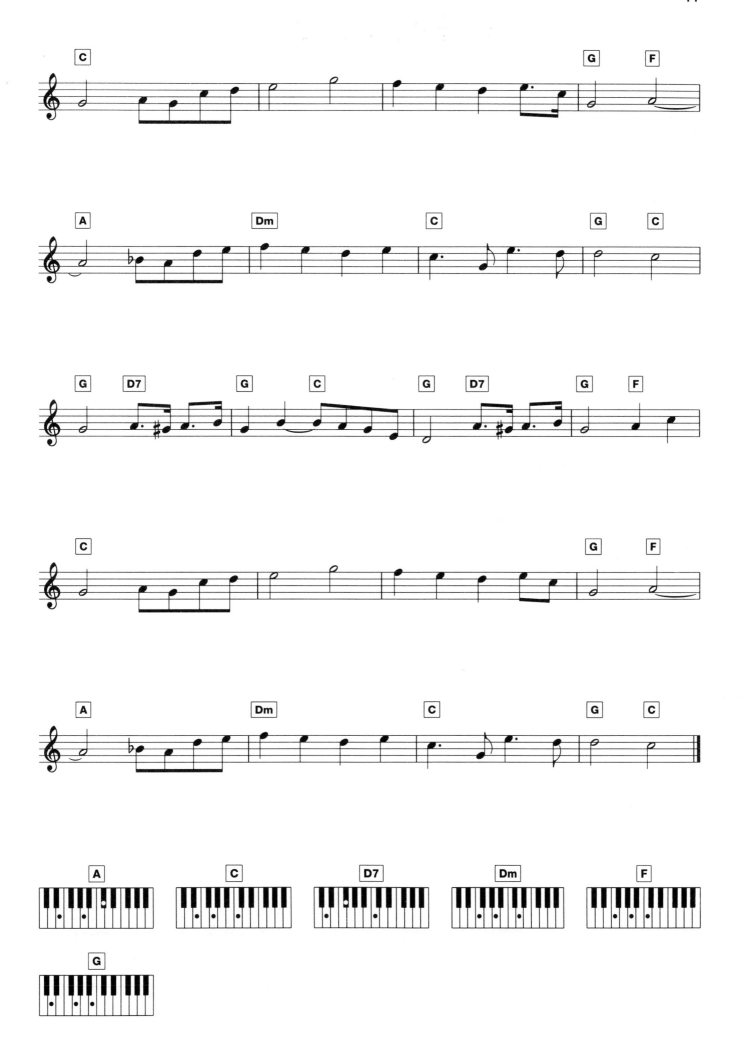

Für Elise

By Ludwig Van Beethoven

Suggested Registration: Piano
Rhythm: Waltz
Tempo: ♩ = 104

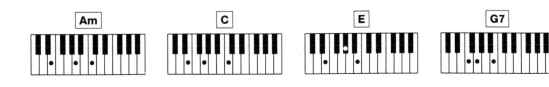

Intermezzo
(From Cavalleria Rusticana)

BANK 22
34
45 - 16+4 org

By Pietro Mascagni

Suggested Registration: Strings
Rhythm: Waltz
Tempo: ♩ = 84

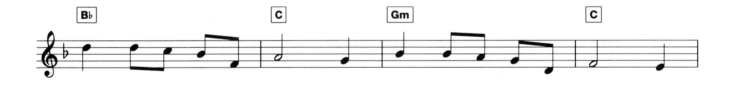

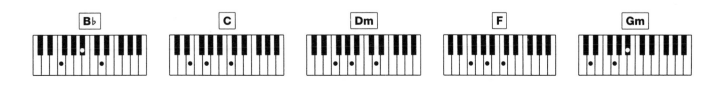

Largo (From New World Symphony)

By Antonín Dvořák

Suggested Registration: Oboe
Rhythm: Soft Rock
Tempo: ♩ = 96

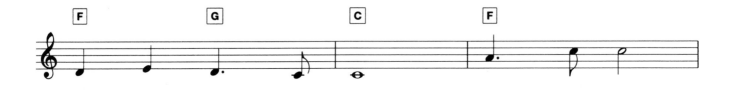

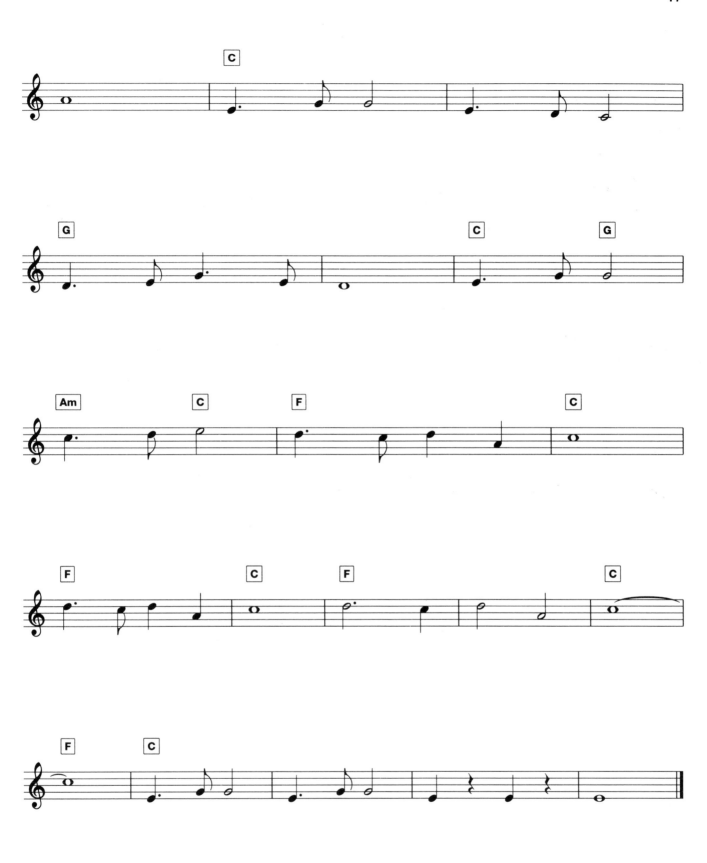

Lullaby

By Johannes Brahms

Suggested Registration: Flute
Rhythm: Waltz
Tempo: ♩ = 92

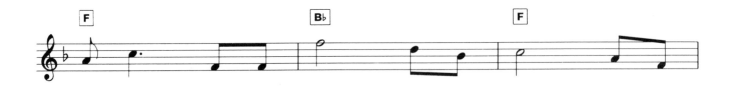

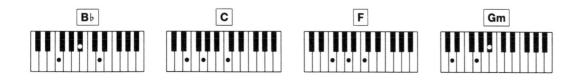

Minuet (From String Quartet)

By Luigi Boccherini

Suggested Registration: Strings
Rhythm: Waltz
Tempo: ♩ = 72

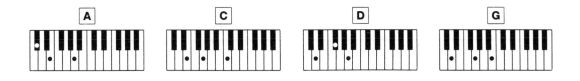

Minuet in G

By Johann Sebastian Bach

Suggested Registration: Harpsichord
Rhythm: Waltz
Tempo: ♩ = 108

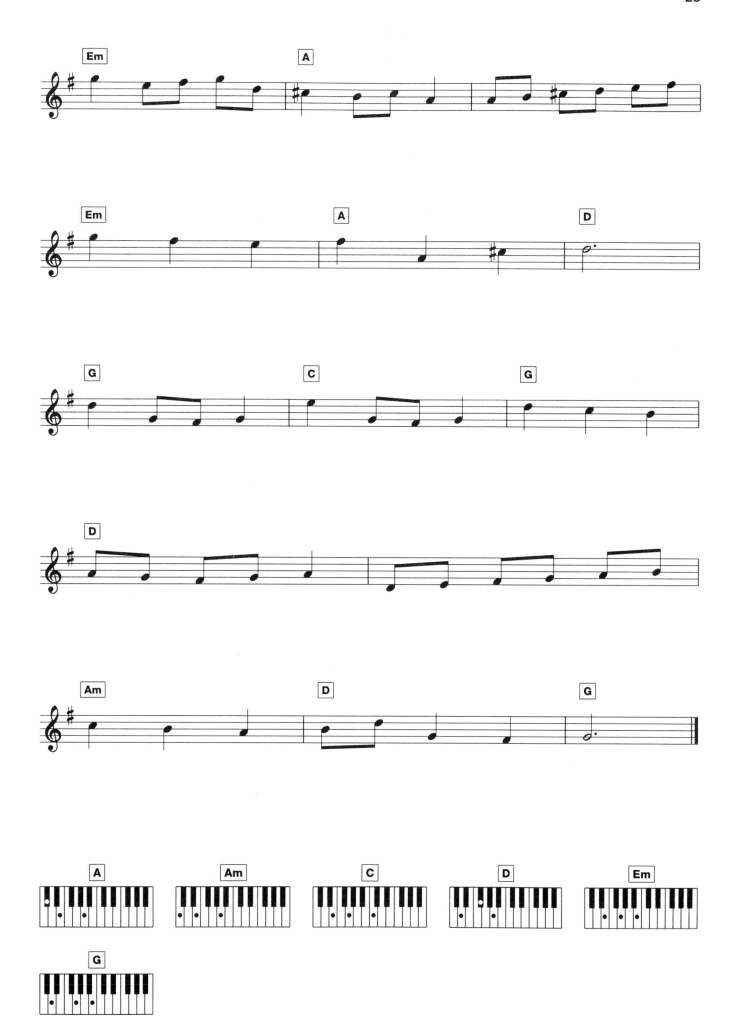

MINUET IN G

By Ludwig Van Beethoven

Suggested Registration: Piano
Rhythm: Waltz
Tempo: ♩ = 96

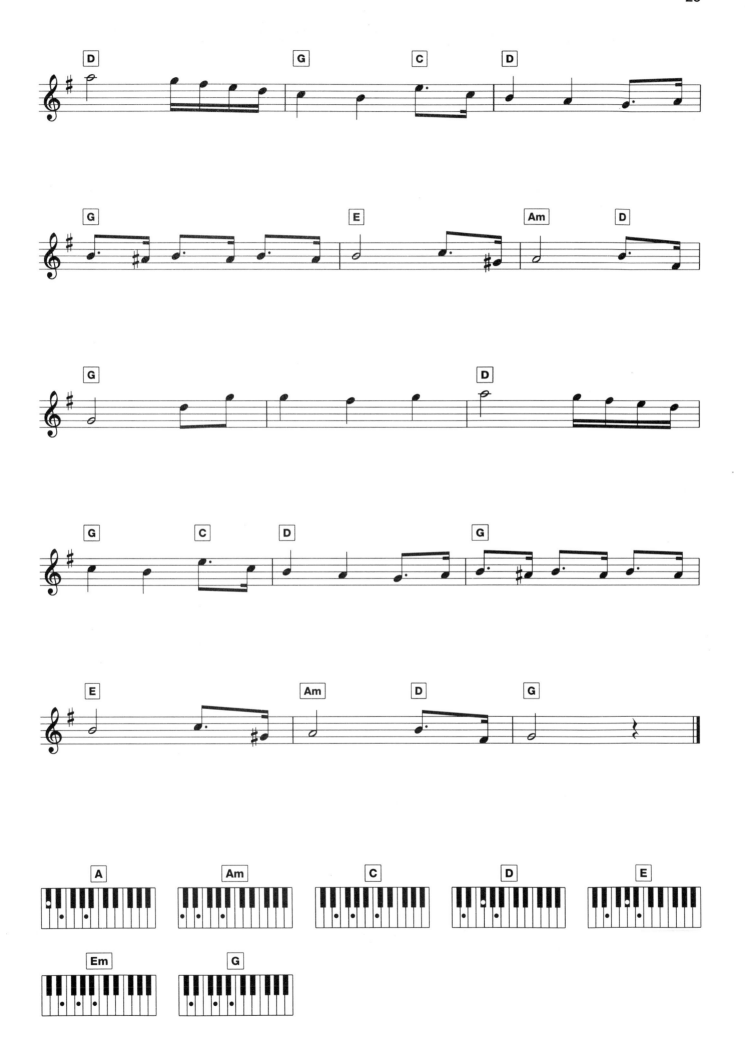

Ode To Joy (From Symphony No 9)

By Ludwig Van Beethoven

Suggested Registration: French Horn
Rhythm: Soft Rock
Tempo: ♩ = 112

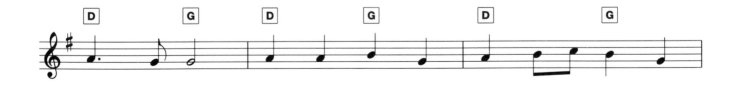

PRELUDE

By Frederic François Chopin

Suggested Registration: Piano
Rhythm: Waltz
Tempo: ♩ = 88

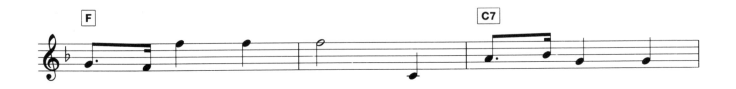

RADETZKY MARCH

By Johann Strauss Snr

Suggested Registration: Clarinet
Rhythm: Slow March
Tempo: ♩ = 84

Spring (From The Four Seasons)

By Antonio Vivaldi

Suggested Registration: Strings
Rhythm: Soft Rock / Baroque
Tempo: ♩ = 176

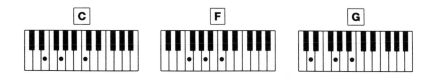

THE SWAN
(FROM CARNIVAL OF THE ANIMALS)

By Charles Camille Saint-Saëns

Suggested Registration: Cello
Rhythm: Waltz
Tempo: ♩ = 80

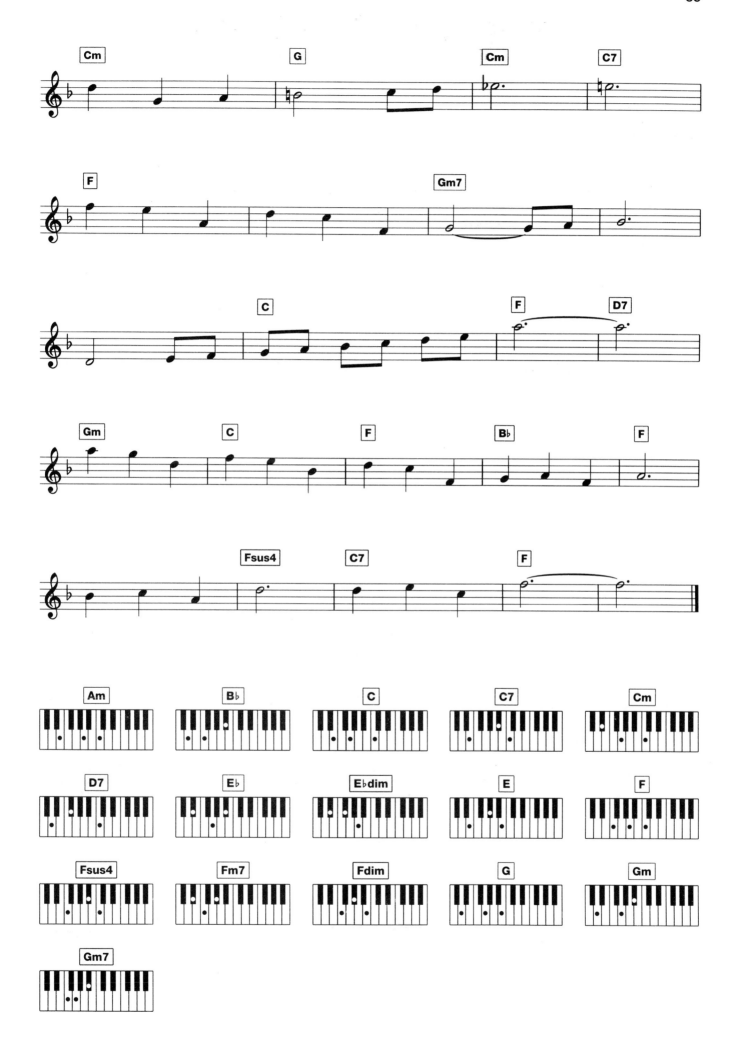

Swan Lake (Main Theme)

By Peter Ilyitch Tchaikovsky

Suggested Registration: Flute
Rhythm: Soft Rock
Tempo: ♩ = 80

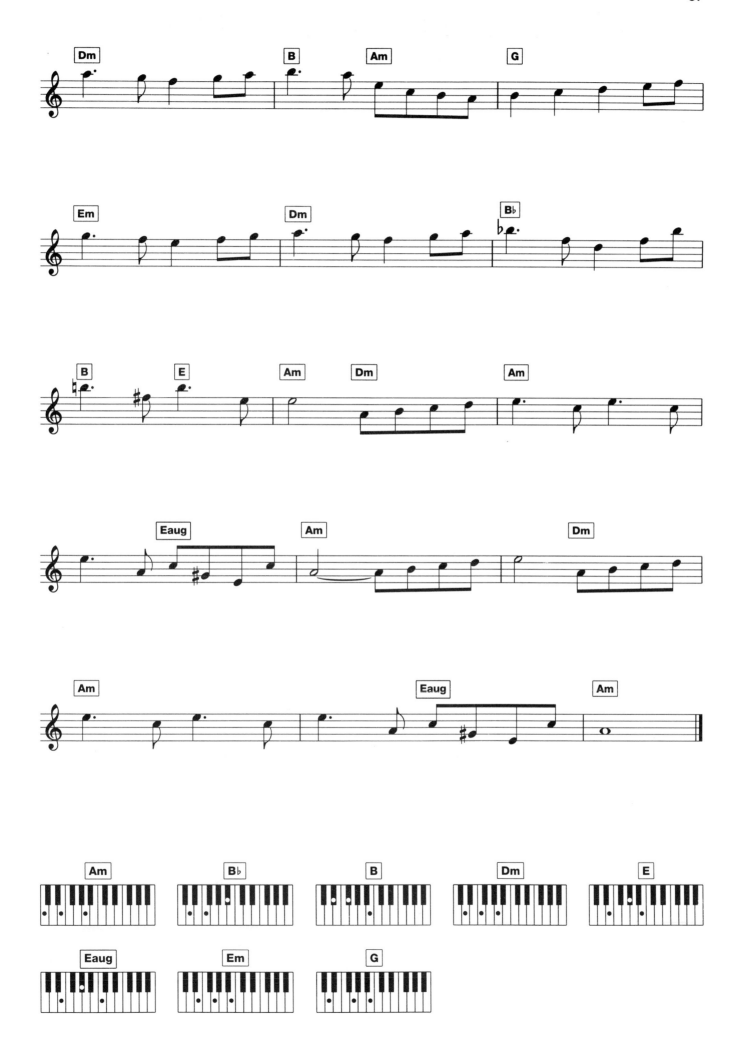

Theme from Symphony No 40

By Wolfgang Amadeus Mozart

Suggested Registration: Strings
Rhythm: 16 Beat
Tempo: ♩ = 88

TO A WILD ROSE
(FROM WOODLAND SKETCHES)

By Edward Alexander MacDowell

Suggested Registration: Piano
Rhythm: Soft Rock
Tempo: ♩ = 72

WALTZ (FROM THE SLEEPING BEAUTY)

By Peter Ilyitch Tchaikovsky

Suggested Registration: Strings
Rhythm: Waltz
Tempo: ♩ = 168

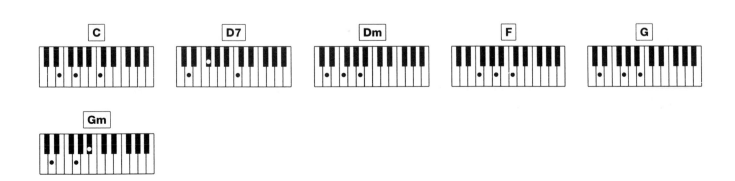

Waves Of The Danube

By Jan Ivanovici

044 RC
145 RC
191 R. H. C. VARIATION

Suggested Registration: Strings
Rhythm: Waltz
Tempo: ♩ = ~~168~~ *120 110*

WILLIAM TELL OVERTURE

By Gioacchina Antonio Rossini

Suggested Registration: Trumpet
Rhythm: March
Tempo: ♩ = 100

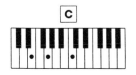
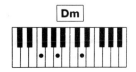
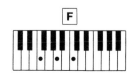
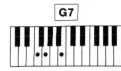

Printed by Watkiss Studios Ltd., Biggleswade, Beds. 02/98

The Easy Keyboard Library Series

Big Band Hits Order Ref: 19098	**Popular Classics** Order Ref: 4180A
Blues Order Ref: 3477A	**Pub Singalong Collection** Order Ref: 3954A
Celebration Songs Order Ref: 3478A	**Rock 'n' Roll Classics** Order Ref: 2224A
Christmas Carols Order Ref: 4616A	**Traditional Scottish Favourites** Order Ref: 4231A
Christmas Songs Order Ref: 19198	**Showtunes - Volume 1** Order Ref: 19103
Classic Hits - Volume 1 Order Ref: 19099	**Showtunes - Volume 2** Order Ref: 3328A
Classic Hits - Volume 2 Order Ref: 19100	**Soft Rock Collection** Order Ref: 4617A
Country Songs Order Ref: 19101	**Soul Classics** Order Ref: 19201
Traditional English Favourites Order Ref: 4229A	**Summer Collection** Order Ref: 3489A
Favourite Hymns Order Ref: 4179A	**TV Themes** Order Ref: 19196
Film Classics Order Ref: 19197	**The Twenties** Order Ref: 2969A
Great Songwriters Order Ref: 2225A	**The Thirties** Order Ref: 2970A
Instrumental Classics Order Ref: 2338A	**The Forties** Order Ref: 2971A
Traditional Irish Favourites Order Ref: 4230A	**The Fifties** Order Ref: 2972A
Love Songs - Volume 1 Order Ref: 19102	**The Sixties** Order Ref: 2973A
Love Songs - Volume 2 Order Ref: 19199	**The Seventies** Order Ref: 2974A
Music Hall Order Ref: 3329A	**The Eighties** Order Ref: 2975A
Motown Classics Order Ref: 2337A	**The Nineties** Order Ref: 2976A
Number One Hits Order Ref: 19200	**Wartime Collection** Order Ref: 3955A

Wedding Collection
Order Ref: 3688A

Exclusive distributors:

International Music Publications Limited
Southend Road, Woodford Green, Essex IG8 8HN
International Music Publications Limited
25 Rue D'Hauteville, 75010 Paris, France
International Music Publications GmbH Germany
Marstallstrasse 8, D-80539 München, Germany
Nuova Carisch S.R.L.
Via M.F. Quintiliano 40, 20138 Milano, Italy
Danmusik
Vognmagergade 7, DK-1120 Copenhagen K, Denmark

EASY KEYBOARD LIBRARY